LEARNING TO LOVE YOURSELF FROM THE INSIDE OUT

INSIDE OUT

A JOURNEY TO A BETTER YOU

Dr. Pam Love

Blessings,
Dr. Love
11/2012

LEARNING TO LOVE YOURSELF FROM THE INSIDE OUT: A JOURNEY TO A BETTER YOU

Printed in the U.S. - Createspace
ISBN-13:978-1478193517
      10:978-1478193514

Cover design by Tiffany Bethea: (www.tiffanybethea.com)
Edited by Nikita Parson

Note to the reader: Information in this book is for educational purposes only. We strive to provide accurate, reliable, and complete information, but do not warrant that this is so.Theauthor is not rendering professional advice. Readers are urged to seek the services of a competent trained professional who provides the services or support desired.No warranties of any kind are expressed or implied. The author and the publisher shall have neither liability nor responsibility to any person or entity with respect to any loss, injury or damage caused, or alleged to have been caused, directly or indirectly, by the information contained in this book. Responsibility for how information in this book is used is solely that of the reader.

Dedication

- To God. Without Him I am nothing.
- To all of the amazing women and men in my life (family, friends, mentors, and mentees). You know who you are.
- To every woman and teen girl who has loved herself in spite of what others have said or tried to do to you!

INTRODUCTION

For many years I didn't think I was good enough or pretty enough or brown enough or shapely enough. I dyed my hair ash blonde, sprayed it red and blue, had all but about 2 inches cut, and wore it twisted for a little more than a year. No matter what I did to my appearance, it was never good enough.

One year, I changed my hair so often that a colleague, who was a therapist, jokingly asked if I needed to be on some type of medication. Although you might think his question to me was rude, it helped me see that others could tell that I was not as happy as I pretended to be. What he and others recognized was that the changes I frequently made to my outer appearance were a reflection of my internal turmoil (i.e. depression and anxiety).

Over the years, I have worn a variety of masks that hid my feelings, talents, and intellect. I didn't want people to see or get to know the "real me". In my mind, being me was too risky. After all, it seemed that each time I was recognized for my academic and social achievements, someone attempted to physically or emotionally hurt me. I was convinced that my life would be easier if I wore a mask and became a follower instead of a leader.

As you can imagine, life didn't get easier. The more I wore my mask, the more frustrated and depressed I became. It wasn't until I got professional help that I realized why I wore a mask, why my self-esteem was low, and why I engaged in self-sabotaging behaviors like drinking, smoking, and risky sexual activity.

A phenomenal therapist helped me take responsibility for my life and reconnect with my emotions. This required me to remove and throw away my mask, become vulnerable, and stop replaying negative messages that I had been telling myself or others told me once or many times. I was almost half way through my forties before I learned how to love myself from the inside out. Now I'm on a mission to help others love themselves and live a life that is far better than they could have imagined.

After releasing my last book, I had the honor of talking with many women at a variety of events. Although I usually couldn't talk long, in the few moments of listening to women, I often learned a lot about their perception of their past and how it had affected their lives. More often than not, women would describe themselves as having "low self-esteem" or would tell a story of a life full of pain, hurt, disappointment, and negative emotions. It was so obvious to me that many of these women hid behind different masks.

For more than a year, people asked if I was going to write a part 2 to my last book, "I Want My Vagina Back." After giving it a lot of thought, I decided that instead of highlighting more of the problem, I would write a book that offers a solution to the problem I saw women struggling with.

That's what this book is all about. ***Learning to Love From The Inside Out: A Journey to A Better You*** was written to help women break free from the struggles of their past and live a life full of love, healthy relationships, and fulfilled dreams.

Sometimes it's difficult to examine your life and make sense of how it may be affecting you. The reality is that you simply don't know what you don't know. There were a number of things about my past that I didn't realize still affected me until my therapist helped me connect some dots. That's why I've included certain information in this book. I hope that it will help you gain insight into why some things have occurred in your life and what it might take for your future to be different than your past. You will explore how your thoughts and emotions might be affecting your behavior and learn how to release anything that keeps you from loving yourself from the inside out.

Completing the exercises in this book might take some time. That's ok, you don't have to rush. If you want to love yourself and have a better life, take your time, give the questions and activities serious thought, and respond from your heart, instead of writing something just to fill in the blanks.

If you have difficulty completing any of the exercises, talk with someone you trust. That person may be able to share something that will be insightful or that jogs your memory about something you've forgotten or suppressed.

In chapters 1-4, I challenge you to explore the power of words and how they may have affected you (chapter 1), to consider which masks you wear (chapter 2), what has influenced your ability to trust (chapter 3), and how your expectations can lead to unhealthy thoughts and responses to others. Chapter 5 gives you an overview of three terms I think are important for you to become familiar with. All three can negatively affect how you feel about yourself and your relationship with others.

I included them because as I've listened to the stories of many women, the picture they painted of their lives (past and present) often included some reference to characteristics of one or more of these terms.

Chapter 6 gives an overview of the importance of something we all need and desire: love. I give you some of the keys to living a life that overflows with an abundance of love.

Finally, chapter 7 includes a number of exercises that can help you not only think about becoming a better you, but take steps that can lead to a life that is better than you can imagine. I've used these exercises for many years and have found them to be very effective. Each exercise will guide you on a path where you can discover the resources, support, and encouragement you need each step of the way.

Learning to Love Yourself From The Inside Out: A Journey to A Better You can change your life for the better. With that in mind, remember that change might take some time. Don't beat yourself up if you feel like you should be farther along in your life. Learn to embrace and celebrate the fact that you're on this journey. Each step you take (small or a quantum leap) moves you closer to where you're supposed to be.

Also remember that your life affects others. Although you may not be responsible for the actions of others (except children or others in your care), what you say and how you live teaches others powerful messages. That's why it's important for you to address life issues and become a better you. If you're going to be an open book for others to read and learn from, make sure you're teaching positive lessons.

Congratulations in advance on your decision to love yourself from the inside out, for choosing to find and reveal your inner beauty, and for each goal you achieve.

My friend, you are beautiful. I believe it, now it's time for you to believe it and live a better life. So turn the pages and let's get started on "...**A Journey to A Better You.**"

Take a deep breath, sit back, and enjoy!

.

TABLE OF CONTENTS

PG

PART I

CHAPTER 1
IT ALL STARTS WITHIN

FAKE WOMAN, THAT'S ME

Fix my hair, paint my toes
Give me more shoes,
purses and clothes.
I need more makeup,
but first fix my lips
Tuck my tummy and
give me curvier hips
I don't care
what you think of me
Just as long as you
like what you see
Cause I'm a woman,
a fake woman,
that's what I'm proud to be!
-PM Love

January 15th

Dear Diary,

I am so excited because I feel really good about myself. My hair is the length I want it to be. It's beautiful. Everyone tells me how pretty my hair is. The other day, my boyfriend wanted to run his fingers through it, but I didn't want him to mess it up especially since I had just gotten it done. My beautician finally gave me a style that complements my face. It makes me feel pretty and sexy. Today is a great hair day!

January 30th

Dear Diary,

I look a hot mess. My beautician took my weave out and I don't feel pretty any more. She didn't want to give me a perm because she said it hadn't been 6 weeks. So she pressed my hair and it was cute until I drove home. It was so humid outside and now I have a curly bush. When I got out of my car, my sister laughed at me and said I needed to get something done to my hair. My boyfriend frowned and said he wouldn't touch my hair 'cuz he didn't want my nappy hair to cut him. I feel ugly today. I don't have $500 to get my weave put back in. I thought about checking my credit card balance or seeing what bill I can pay late. I can't go out looking like this. I'm going to find a way to get my weave put back in and I don't care what I have to do to make that happen. This is not a good hair day and it's messing up my entire day. What am I going to do?

February 2nd

Dear Diary,

I haven't been to work for the last few days. I called and said I was sick. I couldn't go out with my hair looking a mess. I called around yesterday and finally found a stylist that would do my hair for $350. I really can't afford to spend $350, but I can't afford to walk around with bushy hair either. I might just have to pay my son's daycare late. I feel a little guilty because I've spent almost $1,000 in a month on my hair, but I don't know what else to do. I don't have "good hair" like my best friend so I buy hair to make myself look better. I can't stand to look at myself in the mirror most of the time especially when my hair doesn't look good. I don't think there's anything wrong with doing what you have to do to look and feel better. Is there?

PONDER THIS

From the three previous diary entries, we know a few things about the woman: 1) she doesn't feel good about her natural hair; 2) having a weave makes her feel better about how she looks; 3) what others say about her matters; and 4) she spends a lot of money that she says she can't afford to spend.

There is nothing wrong with getting your hair or nails done or doing other things to enhance your appearance. However, it's important to consider your motivation for doing these things. Who and what are you doing these things for? Are you trying to appeal to others or compete with others?

It seems that some women are willing to spend money they can't afford to spend on things that make them feel or look better temporarily. Keep in mind that if you don't feel good about yourself without the enhancements, fixing up your external appearance will only be a temporary fix that will lead to more temporary fixes. No amount of makeup, clothing, or surgery can change the essence of how you feel about yourself.

Until you invest in enhancing the inner you, you will never feel good about your appearance. You may experience degrees of satisfaction, but until you feel that you are a beautiful person on the inside and don't need external validation, you will constantly feel dissatisfied with your "look" and wonder whether it's "good enough."

I am not suggesting that you shouldn't put on makeup, add hair to your natural hair, wear wigs, or get plastic surgery. That's a personal preference and decision. This is about whether you are using enhancements to cover up how you really feel about yourself. Some women think they only look good with long hair. I've heard women say they don't feel attractive because their hair is short. Then there are the women with long hair who complain that their hair is too hard to manage and takes a long time to blow dry. The reality is that whether you have long hair, short hair, a wide nose, freckles, or a large head, it is important for you to realize that beauty begins on the inside (i.e. in the heart and mind). When you learn to accept yourself just as you are, any enhancements you make will be for you. When you love yourself from the inside out, what other people think about your appearance won't affect you in the same way. When you accept yourself and love yourself just as you are, you will free your mind to deal with other things.

Remember that how you honestly feel about yourself positively or negatively affects your mental health which can also affect your physical health. For example, when you are depressed, you might experience headaches, stomach aches, and other physical ailments. That's why it's important to maintain a positive state of mind which includes thinking good thoughts about yourself.

When you love yourself and are not influenced by the opinions and expectations of others, you will step into a level of emotional well-being that is liberating, energizing, and infectious. Loving yourself will cause your true beauty to radiate like the morning sun. Some people might begin to ask you why you're glowing. You'll be able to say "I'm in love.....with myself!"

KEYS FROM THIS CHAPTER

- Feeling good about yourself starts on the inside (in your heart and mind)
- Your feelings affect your emotional and physical well-being
- Thinking good thoughts helps you feel good and radiate beauty from the inside out

TIME TO REFLECT

Can you look at yourself in the mirror for more than a few seconds? ___Yes ___No

If no, why?

Are you comfortable with your appearance when you are in your natural state (no makeup, no extra hair, lashes, natural hair, etc.)? ___Yes ___No

If no, what makes you uncomfortable?

Write down all of the negative words or phrases you use to describe your various features (e.g., skinny legs, huge arms, ugly feet, big nose). You can also write words you think about yourself and don't share with others.

Write down all of the positive words or phrases you use to describe your various features (e.g.

pretty eyes, beautiful hair). You can also write words you think.

Write down the words and phrases (positive and negative) that people have said to you about you or your appearance over the years (e.g., you look nice, you are so skinny; you have some kinky hair, you're smart).

When you look at the list of what you say about yourself or think about yourself (positive and negative) and what others have said to you, how much of those words and thoughts do you think have affected how you feel about yourself?

How much of your thoughts and words and the words of others do you think has affected how much time you spend making yourself appear a certain way?

CHAPTER 2
COME FROM BEHIND THE
MASK YOU'RE WEARING

I AM HUMAN

I am human just like you.
Take me off that pedestal,
I make mistakes too.
Please stop, don't look at me.
Your eyes are on the wrong person
they're not where they should be
I'm tired of pretending
Acting like everything is ok
Just accept that I make mistakes
And don't monitor
every word that I say.
PM Love

February 11th

Dear Diary,

I had a great time in church today. The message was inspirational and really spoke to me. Pastor preached on the virtuous woman. I've heard it preached many times, but he said some things I'd never thought about.

I think Pastor's message ministered to me because I really do desire to be a virtuous woman. I think I'm a good mother, friend, and generally good to most people. The challenge is that most people don't get to see the "real" me because I wear a lot of masks. I know how to use all of the "right" words so that people believe what I say. I also know how to fix myself up so that I look good on the outside. I wear a mask when I'm around co-workers and friends. What else can I do? I don't want others to know how unhappy I am. I'm tired of being single. I'm tired of occasionally having sex, feeling guilty then vowing that I'm going to wait until I'm married to have sex again. I wish I could talk to one of the women in the church, but I can't because a lot of them are judgmental.

I went to women's ministry one time and it was a turnoff. Whenever there was a question about sex, there was always some "holier than thou" woman reminding the women of the 8 years she's been abstinent. Good for her. I don't want to be abstinent that long. I want to have sex. I have had sex, I like sex, and I want to have more sex. I do want to be married when I have sex, but since I'm not even dating, I don't know when or if I'll ever get married. So what am I supposed to do to satisfy my needs? I've tried toys and even slept with a woman. Both felt good. I didn't want a relationship with the woman. It was one of those things that I was curious about, tried it, and got pleasure from.

I tried to bring this up in bible study and again in women's ministry. I talked about "a woman I know." Thank God I didn't say I was talking about myself. As soon as I brought up the subject of women being attracted to other women, two of the leaders threw scriptures at me and said that "lesbians who claim to be Christians are weak women who have chosen to yield to the flesh and will be condemned to hell unless they stop." One of them said that women like that need to pray, meditate daily on scripture, and in a matter of days, they wouldn't be attracted to women any longer.

I pray and I read scripture, but I still struggle. My desires are real and I'm tired of pretending that they don't exist. Even now, as I sit at my computer typing, I'm thinking about tuning in to one of the chat rooms where you go for cybersex.

What do I do? I don't feel good about myself. I'm unhappy, frustrated, tired of acting fake and phoney and tired of being around people who are fake and phoney. I wish I had someone I could talk to.

PONDER THIS

Many women wear a mask so that others don't get to see who they really are. A mask gives people a picture of who you are, but it is a picture that you have created. It's not you.

Behind a mask are expressions, thoughts, and feelings that often go unnoticed. If you could turn people inside out and see their thoughts, you might be quite surprised to discover how different they are than how they appear or what they say. For instance, someone told the story of a woman who came to work one day and seemed just as jovial as she normally was. She laughed and joked with her co-workers and customers, bought one co-worker lunch and gave her several dresses that she had never worn. From what everyone could tell, she was fine. Later that evening, the woman committed suicide. She left a note saying she wanted someone to notice how much pain she was in, but no one stopped to look beyond her smiles and laughs. The note, sent to one of her coworkers by email, stated that her husband had been beating her for more than 3 months. She wrote that she was tired of pretending everything was ok. She couldn't take his verbal and physical abuse anymore. She didn't want any more of his gifts and trinkets. She wished someone had noticed how much makeup she wore and could see the bald spots under her wigs from where he pulled patches of her hair out. This woman closed her letter by saying she hopes others will pay more attention to one another. She hoped no one else would die without someone seeing their pain.

Like so many women, this woman was crying inside, but no one could see the tears behind the mask she wore every day. Some women say it's easier to pretend than it is to show people how frustrated, tired, worried, and unhappy they are. Others say they don't want to bother people with their "stuff". Instead, they carry their negative emotions around like a bag of rocks stuffed in their purse. They learn to adjust their body and facial expressions and don't ask for help when the weight is more than they can bear.

What about you? Do you wear masks to hide how you feel and what's going on in your life? If you answered yes, you're not alone.

However, understand that when you wear a mask, you're denying yourself an opportunity to demonstrate love and concern for yourself. You're denying others an opportunity to help you deal with your emotions or whatever you're dealing with.

When I talk about wearing a mask, I'm not talking about an occasional smile when you're upset or walking into a meeting and acting like everything is ok when you're going through issues at home. There are appropriate and inappropriate times to display emotions and behaviors. What I'm referring to is when you continue to deny how you truly feel or intentionally behave in a manner that causes others to have a certain perception of you that is not true. It's not healthy to ignore your emotions and feelings. They are signals to your mind and body just as a stop sign or red light serve as signals for drivers. What you may not realize is that when you suppress or ignore your emotions and feelings, they don't go away. What happens is that they will manifest in some other way. As previously mentioned, your emotional state affects you physically. Whenever I visited my former primary care doctor and described physical symptoms, he always asked what was going on in my life. You see, my doctor recognized that when I was stressed or feeling somewhat depressed, it caused me to get sick. I once read a statement by Dr. Don Colbert that I might never forget. In Dr. Colbert's book, he wrote that he "was tired of seeing people weep through their skin." People were coming to him with eczema and other conditions and he like others discovered that some conditions clear up or are better managed after the patients address the issues that cause them to feel stressed, unloved, unappreciated, angry, etc. Are you "weeping through your skin" or experiencing some other health conditions because you're not dealing with your emotions?

In the diary entry at the beginning of this chapter, the woman wrote about how she pretends to be abstaining from sex when she's around her church members, but privately has engaged in sex with males and females. She wants to tell others how she feels and how ashamed and guilty she feels at times. She wants someone to talk with someone, but it seems that she hasn't found anyone who she feels comfortable enough to remove her mask. So she keeps wearing it instead of removing it.

Whether it's sex, drug use, or people that result in you experiencing negative emotions and feelings, love yourself enough to find someone who can help you deal with your truth and take off your mask. I know that some people will judge you, give you advice that is meaningless to you, and some people may not understand what you're going through or how to help you. However, there are still a lot of people who are trustworthy, who won't criticize you, and who will give you sound guidance to help you learn to love yourself and live without a mask. Consider the following options:

1) Talk with a trained professional (e.g. a therapist or counselor) who has the resources and objectivity to help you work through your issues; or

2) Talk with someone who genuinely cares for you like a pastor, minister, rabbi, mentor, or life coach. Although they may not be qualified to provide therapy, they may be able to talk with you about your issues and give you that safe

place you need to be vulnerable without feeling judged or ashamed.

On this journey as you learn to love yourself, you must learn to trust yourself. As you learn to trust yourself, you will discern who you can/cannot trust. Trusting yourself will also help you take off your mask and never want to put it on again. It doesn't mean you won't put it on, but once you've taken it off, putting it back on will never feel the same again. This takes time. So don't try to rush yourself. Masks don't get created overnight and may not come off immediately, but when they do come off, don't be surprised if you actually feel like a 50 pound weight has been lifted off of you.

🗝 KEYS FROM THIS CHAPTER

🗝 Removing your mask is a step toward revealing your authentic self

🗝 Learning to trust yourself involves knowing yourself

🗝 Removing your mask has emotional and physical benefits

TIME TO REFLECT

Circle all of the masks that you currently wear and put an X through all of the masks you have worn at any point in your life:

The **"I'm doing ok"** mask (when you're really not ok emotionally or physically)

The **"I'm so happy for you"** mask (when you're struggling with feeling happy for someone else and wonder when something good will happen in your life)

The **"I don't care what people think about me"** mask (when you really do care and are easily offended)

The **"I've got it going on financially, in my relationship, and/or how I feel about myself"** mask (when things aren't as good as others think)

The **"I like you"** mask (when you really don't care to be around the person)

The **"I believe things will be ok"** mask (when you are worrying and doubting that things will be ok.).

What   other   mask   have   you   worn?

_____

Are you able to be around people you're close to without wearing a mask? Why or why not?

Do you know if the women you're connected to can be around you without wearing a mask? How do you know this?

If a woman confided in you that she was watching pornography, how would you respond? Would your response be different if she was married and watched it with her husband?

Which of the following words do you think describes how you would respond to the lady in the previous question? Circle as many as apply.

from my heart   compassionate

empathic   understanding

self-centered   Direct

judgmental   rigid   harsh

self righteous   loving   no response

Other (describe) _____

Ask a woman you're close to (who will be honest with you), which of the words above describes how she believes you would respond to the woman who says she watches pornography with or without her husband..

Did the woman you asked have a response that was similar or different than yours? Were you surprised at any of the words she selected?

Self-awareness is critical to personal growth. Knowing how you respond to others can help you learn more about yourself and how to effectively respond to others from your authentic self. We often say it's important to "speak the truth." That might feel good in the moment, but being direct or harsh or judgmental may not help others feel they can be honest with you. Instead of simply speaking what you feel, consider what's more important: speaking your truth or listening to the other person and responding in a way that is helpful. Words are powerful. Therefore, what you say and the spirit behind what you say is critical.

Consider the tone you use, your body language, and what you say when responding to others. As you become more aware of how you respond to others, you are also teaching others how to interact with you, who you are, and how you operate without a mask. You're also learning how to have healthier informal and formal relationships with others. You're learning to be *a better you*!

CHAPTER 3

LEARNING TO TRUST

WHY TRUST?

Why should I trust you?

What do you have to say?

'Cuz momma said

all men cheat any ole way.

You're just like the others

Why should I believe your lies?

I know you're up to no good

Sooner or later you'll make me cry.

-PM Love

February 19th

Dear Diary:

It seems like every relationship I get in, ends because I can't trust the other person. Every guy either cheats on me or leaves me to be with someone else. In some cases, I end the relationship before anything happens because I know sooner or later, something will happen. It's just like my mother always told me: You can't trust a man. Men will be men. She frequently reminded me about the time my father left us. Momma said I should always keep my eyes open so I don't get blindsided like she did. I tried not to believe my mother, but it seems like she's right. Maybe I just need to be by myself. I wonder if therapy would help. Never mind, that won't help. I've been struggling with this for a long time. I just think men can't be trusted. That's what my momma said and I believe her because she doesn't have a reason to lie to me.

PONDER THIS

Many women describe relationships in which trust is a major issue. What is interesting in the previous diary entry is that this woman attributes what happens in the relationships to the men she dates. She doesn't seem to take responsibility for the part she might have played in her relationships. She may not realize how much of her feelings about men and how she responds in a relationship might be the result of what her momma told her. It's clear that she keeps replaying in her mind what her mother told her about men and her mantra has become "don't trust men."

As mentioned in an earlier chapter, self-awareness is a very important part of the process of learning to live authentically and with joy and fulfillment. As you discover more about yourself, it may help to understand how past experiences and what people have said to you may be affecting how you feel about yourself and how you interact with others.

Well-intentioned women often say things to one another out of their own hurt and frustration. Some advice comes from a culmination of past experiences or experiences of others. This is critical because advice that is based on opinions and emotions is simply advice that we believe to be true, but may not be the truth. When a woman tells her daughter that men can't be trusted, that's her mother's opinion. That is not the truth. Although some men may not be trustworthy, it's wrong to make a generalization like "you can't trust any man." Those types of opinions and generalizations can damage your ability to have a healthy relationship.

Be aware of the ways in which your past, including messages from others, affects your beliefs, feelings, and actions. In the case of the woman in the diary entry whose father left her mother, it is possible that as an adult, she may experience symptoms associated with having been abandoned by her father when she was a child. I will talk more about this in chapter 5.

Whether it's abandonment or something else, gaining a better understanding of who you are, how your past continues to affect you, and how you interact with others is an important part of your growing, maturing, and having healthy relationships.

Trust is something that comes from within. You must first learn to trust yourself. What does that mean? It means you learn to become comfortable with your thoughts, feelings, decisions, and actions. This takes practice and also requires you to have others around you to help you in this process. Why? There are times that messages and experiences from your past or your emotions will influence your ability to make good decisions. There also may be times when your hormones might be out of balance or you could be experiencing mental or physical health issues that affect your thoughts, decisions, and actions. That's why it is helpful to have people around you that you can trust to give you wise counsel and aren't afraid of telling you when your decisions may not be in your best interest or in the best interest of others. As you learn to trust yourself, you will begin to have healthier and more rewarding relationships with others.

Learning to trust yourself doesn't mean you do things in isolation. It requires you to know yourself and become confident in your ability to gather enough good data to make informed or wise decisions.

When faced with the need to make a decision to do something like go on a date with a man who you don't have good feelings about, trust your instincts and consider talking with someone you trust. That person can help you determine if the feelings you're having are because of past experiences, fear of being rejected or hurt, or if there could be something about him that you're attracted to (e.g. he's very take charge) that might not be good for you. By trusting yourself and/or consulting with a friend, you might decide that this "take charge" behavior reminds you of your mother's behavior. As you observe the gentleman a little more, you're able to confirm that just like your mom, he's controlling. Instead of going out with him, you politely decline and move on. Save yourself some time and aggravation by learning to trust yourself and the wise counsel of others.

As you learn to trust yourself, keep in mind that everyone makes mistakes. So you can expect that at some point, you might make a bad decision or do something that you regret. When that happens, remember that making mistakes is normal. Mistakes are great opportunities for learning how to improve or make better decisions in the future. Let yourself off the hook *when* you make a mistake (if it was not done with malice or intentionally to harm someone). Talk with someone you trust about the mistake and then work to move forward knowing that you have the capability to make good decisions in the future.

Note: If you have been diagnosed with a mental health disorder or have a physical illness, consult your doctor regarding the ways in which your condition and any medications you are taking might affect your ability to focus and make healthy, affirming decisions.

🗝 KEYS FROM THIS CHAPTER

- 🗝 Words that you receive and believe can impact you for many years.
- 🗝 Shifting your beliefs and gathering good information, can help you make wise decisions.
- 🗝 Making mistakes is normal. They can teach you important life lessons

TIME TO REFLECT

In what area(s) of your life are you having difficulty?

Circle all of the following issues that you have been dealing with recently or that you periodically deal with:

anxiety   low self-esteem

bad relationship(s)   anger

unforgiveness   guilt   shame

an addiction (to food, sex, alcohol, drugs, etc.)

Whose voice or words of "advice" do you think about most often?

What advice have you been given that may not have been the best advice for you?

CHAPTER 4

EXPECTATIONS AREN'T ENTITLEMENTS

EXPECTATIONS

I DESERVE THE BEST,
I EXPECT WHAT I DESIRE
I SHALL HAVE WHAT I WANT,
BEFORE I RETIRE
I EXPECT IT FROM YOU,
I'M NOT ACCEPTING ANYTHING LESS
IF YOU DON'T MEET MY DEMANDS,
IT IS YOU I'M GOING TO DETEST!
PM Love

February 22nd

Dear Diary,

I told him before we got married that I wanted a
4 bedroom house with a 3-car garage, a pool
out back, an S-class Mercedes, and no more
than 2 children who I would stay home and
take care of until they went to middle school. I
told him. I accepted that we couldn't afford for
me to stay home after the first child. I accepted
that the house didn't have a pool and I even
was willing to drive a Honda for a few years.
But it has been 2 years and I think I'm done.
I'm pregnant with our second child and my
husband is saying we still can't afford for me to
stay home to raise our children. My Honda is 3
years old and my husband told me that if I give
him 2 more years, I can have my S-class
Mercedes. We used my money and money
from my parents to buy this house. I make
more money than my husband, but that's
because I have a salary plus commission. Just
like I work my tail off to get big bonuses, he
could do the same or get a second job. I work
hard and I deserve to have the things I want. I
don't feel like he's helping move us closer to
my dreams. This isn't working for me. I told him

what I wanted. He knew what he was getting into when we got married. I know God hates divorce, but I'll just ask for His forgiveness because I don't know if I can keep living like this. I deserve better and I know better is out there for me.

PONDER THIS

It is important to know what you want and express it. However, in a relationship, there should be some level of compromise. If you feel like you have to get everything you want and have everything go your way, you are being selfish. That's right, I said it. You are acting like a small child who wants the world and all the people in it to meet her needs and nothing else matters. Does that describe you at times? The other extreme of being selfish is being unselfish without balance. If you are always sacrificing your needs to meet the needs of others, that is unhealthy. If you are constantly doing for others because you are concerned about them rejecting you or having negative feelings toward you, that is unhealthy. Is that what you've been doing?

If you're going to love yourself unconditionally and learn to have healthy relationships, it is important for you to learn how to set boundaries, acknowledge and express your feelings, and create some sort of balance between being selfish and sacrificing your needs for others.

You should also be realistic about your expectations. It's one thing to set expectations for yourself. However, be careful about imposing your expectations on others unless you hire them to do work for you, supervise them, or are training them. In relationships (whether it's with a parent, partner, spouse, friend, etc.), communicate your expectations, but don't assume that they will always be met.

In the diary entry, the woman is upset because she told her husband how she expected to live and what she wanted once they got married (i.e. a house, Mercedes, and being a stay at home mom, etc.). When those expectations aren't met, she gets angry and upset. It's not good enough for her to have a house, a car, and money to take care of their children. Her life isn't fitting the picture she created in the timeframe she planned. Her diary entry reflects someone who is being a little selfish.

Even when you've talked about your expectations with the person you're in a relationship with, it's important that you recognize things might not occur exactly when and how you expect them to happen. Also be aware of when you have gone from having expectations to feeling entitled. A sense of entitlement can be harmful to relationships.

In the diary entry, the woman says she "deserves" certain things. Your feelings about what you deserve are just that – your feelings. Just because you feel like you deserve something, doesn't mean that that's true. Although there are certain things you absolutely deserve from others like respect and love, be careful about assuming that others have a responsibility to meet your expectations (unless it's in an employment type situation or when raising children).

Many of us go through life feeling like we deserve more or better than what we have. We become obsessed with getting "more", whether that *more* is money, a home, car, or a lifestyle that equals or exceeds people we know.

As we search deep within our souls, we should consider the "why" of what we want. Why do you expect to have and do what you desire? What makes you feel you deserve a promotion? What if you get it and it turns out to be a nightmare position? Do you still deserve it or will you feel like you deserve something better? Just like wearing makeup and getting plastic surgery doesn't give you a permanent boost to your self esteem, getting what you want or having things go your way is not always healthy for you and may not be good if you're in a relationship.

Think about your expectations for a minute. Consider what you want to be, do, and have over the next 5-10 years. Why do you really want what you expect to have in the future? In some cases, our expectations are rooted in fear and selfishness. In other cases, our wants are rooted in competition. We simply want to "keep up with the Jones family".

Let me caution you because while you're working hard to give others the impression that you're living a certain lifestyle, you might end up creating more stress in your life. Too many people have purchased homes and cars and furniture they couldn't afford, but felt they deserved. Juggling bills, responding or ignoring creditors, hoping there's no eviction or foreclosure notice on your front door, or hiding your car so it doesn't get repossessed are just a few of the outcomes that can occur if you really can't afford to keep up with the Joneses. Before you purchase anything, consider whether 1) you're creating debt you can't afford at the time; 2) it's an impulse buy or something you want to impress others; 3) you are about to use your money wisely.

Many people are trying to fulfill the expectations of parents or other family members. Parents have a way of placing expectations on children that children do their best to live up to. Employers do the same thing. Because they're trying to meet certain goals, they place expectations on you. In both cases (parents and employers), it is fine for them to place their expectations on you as long as you understand how those expectations affect you and how you feel about yourself and your life. Remember, learning to love yourself is all about acknowledging, embracing, and celebrating your authentic self. So without any masks on, examine expectations that others have for you and make sure they won't cause you to put another mask on. If they do, consult a trusted friend or trained professional to help you figure out what you need to do to have a life without a mask and one that is full of love.

⚷ KEYS FROM THIS CHAPTER

- ⚷ Expectations are not entitlements
- ⚷ Healthy relationships involve compromise and not selfishness
- ⚷ Living up to the expectations of others doesn't give you room to live your own life.

TIME TO REFLECT

What is your ideal lifestyle (amount of money you make, type of car you want, type of home you want to live in; vacation, etc.?

If you are married, have you and your spouse discussed your ideal lifestyle? What about what you want to do or have in 5 or 10 years? Why or why not? If you're not married, when do you think is the best time for you to share with a potential mate what you hope your life with a husband will be like?

Can you identify the source of your expectations and whether they're rooted in fear, love, or something else? For instance, some people who have been poor will strive to never be in poverty again. So they will have an expectation that the bank account or funds they can access quickly, should never go below a certain amount. When the funds get low, it can create anxiety. In this situation, the person's expectation would be based in fear.

List 3 of your expectations and see if you can identify the source or basis for each expectation. You can list a relationship expectation like: I expect my husband to allow me to take care of the finances. Or list an expectation for yourself. A lady once said that she had to have a closet full of shoes. That expectation came from her being poor as a child, only having one pair of shoes, and being embarrassed when she had to wear shoes with holes in them.

CHAPTER 5
HOW YOUR PAST MIGHT BE AFFECTING YOU NOW

WHEN YOUR PAST IS STILL THE PROBLEM

YOU WERE A CHILD WHEN HE LEFT YOUR MOM AND WHEN SHE STOPPED ACTING LIKE YOU EXISTED

NOW YOU'RE OLDER AND YOU STRUGGLE IN RELATIONSHIPS, YOU'RE NOT SURE WHY THEY ALL GET THINGS TWISTED

MOM WAS AN ADDICT AND LEFT YOU HOME TO CARE FOR YOUR SISTERS AND BROTHERS

NOW YOU'RE OLDER AND YOU'RE TIRED OF FEELING TAKEN ADVANTAGE OF, YOU'RE TIRED OF ALWAYS BEING THERE FOR OTHERS

THE REASON FOR SOME OF YOUR PRESENT STRUGGLES MIGHT HAVE TO DO WITH THINGS FROM YOUR PAST

ONCE YOU MAKE THE CONNECTION AND ADDRESS THEM, YOU MIGHT FEEL BETTER AND HAVE A RELATIONSHIP THAT LASTS!

-PM Love

March 4, 2012

Dear Diary,

People make me sick. I don't trust anyone anymore. They claim to care about me, but all they do is take advantage of me. I'm so tired of taking care of everybody else and nobody takes care of me. I'm sick of people. They call me when they need money, when they need a place to stay, and to use my car. I keep giving and all people do is use me and walk away. I think I need to be by myself, that way I don't have to deal with people. I'm just sick of people.

POINTS TO PONDER

By now you should have thought a lot about who you are, your thoughts, and whether or not you wear masks to hide your authentic self from others. In this chapter, I discuss 3 concepts that affect many people and their relationships: 1. **Abandonment** (which I will call "The Trust Buster"), **2. Codependency** (which I call the "I Can Save the World

Syndrome"), and **3. parentification** (which I call "The Child Is the Parent Syndrome"). These concepts represent issues that affect females and males, but for purposes of this book, I refer only to females in my description. I selected these concepts because when many women that I've spoken with tell me about issues they're struggling with and some of the things that have occurred in their past, more often than not, one of these terms is relevant.

At the beginning of this chapter, the woman's diary entry suggests that she displays characteristics associated with abandonment, codependency or parentification. After reading the description of each term, see if you can identify which one(s) she describes.

Abandonment, codependency, and parentification can impact how you respond to people who are close to you or attempt to get close to you, your ability to make good decisions, and the quality of your relationships.

All three can also affect your self-esteem and your ability to love yourself and others.

As you review each term, try to refrain from thinking about others. See if any of the descriptions apply to you. If after reading each description you don't understand what one or more terms mean, search the internet or go to a library or bookstore. There is an abundance of material available that can increase your understanding and give you greater insight into the ways in which each concept may or may not be relevant to you.

Concepts you should be familiar with:

Abandonment (a.k.a. the"**Trust Buster**")– occurs when someone (usually a parent or guardian) leaves you (e.g. dad or mom moves out or suddenly stops coming around to pick you up or spend time with you) or withholds their love and affection from you (e.g. doesn't hug you or instead of expressing positive emotions, says negative things about you).

Impact of the "Trust Buster": being emotionally or physically abandoned can cause you to feel rejected and emotionally or physically "abandoned." Throughout your life, you might struggle with feelings of insecurity. As an adult, it may be difficult for you to be vulnerable and trust people who attempt to get close to you. You may fear that s/he will leave you. Consequently, you may do things to push the person away before s/he leaves or hurts you. Look at the following example:

Lisa's father left her and her mother when Lisa was 12 years old. Lisa thought that she and her mom were better off not having her dad around because he struggled with an addiction and was in and out of prison most of Lisa's life. However, Lisa has often wondered what it would have been like to have her dad around at least for her birthday, graduation, and other special occasions. Lisa is 23 years old and feels she has done just fine without having her dad in her life.

Lisa has been dating Joseph for 6 months. Lisa told Joseph that her birthday was Tuesday and that she was having a birthday celebration at a restaurant on Friday evening. Joseph assures her he will be there. Everyone except Joseph arrived at the restaurant by 7:30pm. Lisa tried to pretend that she wasn't upset that Joseph never showed up. She got up to "go to the bathroom" a few times, but stepped outside to call Joseph. Since he didn't answer, Lisa got angry. During her last call to Joseph at 9:30 pm., Lisa left a voice message expressing how upset she was over him not coming to her celebration. Further, she told Joseph that their relationship was over and that he shouldn't call her ever again. Joseph called Lisa at 11:45pm, 12:00 a.m., and 1:00 a.m. and continued to call until the next morning, but Lisa refused to answer his calls. When she decided to answer at 11 a.m. the next day, Joseph told her how sorry he was for missing her celebration, but *that he was in the hospital after being in a major car accident.*

    This might seem like an extreme situation, but it represents the magnitude of the response one may experience because of situations that cause feelings that trigger emotions related to being abandoned in the past.

Codependency (a.k.a. *"I Can Save the World" syndrome*) – According to Mental Health America (as described at www.mentalhealthamerica.net), codependency is also known as a relationship addiction. It is a "learned behavior of people who live with or have been in a relationship with someone with an addiction or a mental illness. The co-dependent person sacrifices her needs to care for the addict or person who is ill.

Impact of codependency: By placing the needs of others before her own, a codependent person can lose sight of her own needs, desires, and sense of self. It can result in low self-esteem and the need to seek approval from others; to be hard on yourself when you make a mistake; exhibit compulsive behaviors like unhealthy sexual activity, addictions, and becoming a workaholic. Codependency can also lead to fear of abandonment, anger, lying, and a tendency to consistently go over and beyond when asked to do something. Let's look at an example:

Janae's father was an alcoholic. He also had a gambling addiction. Dad would come home late some nights and take things out of the house to sell so he could have more money to gamble and spend on drinks. Janae spent many mornings cleaning up after her dad vomited before he could get into the bathroom. Because he would be too hung over to go to work, he would ask Janae to call his job and make up some excuse for him. He told Janae to do whatever it took so that he didn't lose his job. Janae learned to make up lies and even got a friend whose dad was a doctor to steal some blank sick slips from her dad that Janae would fill out, sign, and fax to her dad's job when they asked for them. Janae's mom also encouraged Janae to help her dad out.

When Janae turned 20, she moved out of her parents' home. She found herself always helping other people with their problems even when it meant neglecting herself. She also realized that she attracted men who had some type of addiction. In each relationship, Janae lied for men and did things that she was so ashamed of, but felt it was her responsibility to help them. Janae didn't realize how much she enabled others until a close friend invited her to attend a support group for family members of addicts.

Codependency can be just as unhealthy as an addiction. In a lot of cases, this "I Can Save the World" syndrome leads to behaviors that mirror addicts. Enabling others (e.g., your adult child keeps losing his job and you keep paying his bills until he gets another job), doesn't really "help" the person. In the long run, important lessons are not learned by the addict and you will end up possibly more frustrated and in a continuous cycle of unhealthy relationships.

Parentification (a.k.a. the **"Child Becomes the Parent" syndrome**) – occurs when there is a role reversal between a parent and a child. The child sacrifices his/her needs to care for the needs of a parent. This can happen when a parent is sick alot, is emotionally unstable, or experiences ongoing stress. If the parent encourages his/her child (directly or indirectly) to provide ongoing support, do something to minimize the negative feelings of the parent, or expects the child to take care of him/her, the child learns to take on the role of the parent. For instance, when a mother is depressed, if the child hears her mom crying, the child may worry about the parent, constantly check in to make sure the parent is ok, and do things to try and help her mother feel better. When children learn to take care of a parent/guardian, it affects the child's ability to feel and express emotions normally.

It is not the role of a child to take care of a parent emotionally or physically. When that happens, it doesn't allow the child to be a child and go through normal stages of emotional development.

Impact of parentification: Parentified children can become angry adults or can have difficulty having healthy, satisfying, and loving relationships. Whenever someone shares his/her expectations with the adult (e.g. A boyfriend says: "I really wanted you to cancel your meeting and stay home with me") that triggers memories of her parent's behavior (e.g. mom used to ask the child to stay in the house in case she got sick and needed something instead of allowing the child to go outside and play with her friends), it can cause passive or explosive anger for the adult who may or may not realize her feelings are tied to her past. Let's look at an example:

Tonya's dad and mom divorced when Tonya was 13 years old. Tonya had 3 younger siblings that her father told her to make sure she helped take care of. Tonya's mom, who had never worked before the divorce, found a job and started working 10-12 hours per day. At some point, she told Tonya "You're in charge. You get to be the woman of the house while I'm not around." Over time, Tonya made sure her mom's bath water was run when she got in at night and heated dinner for her mom after getting her siblings to bed. Tonya looked forward to her mom coming home. She'd tell her to call when she was on her way home and to let her know when she was close to the house. Because her mom often complained about her feet hurting, Tonya used money she planned to use for herself on a foot massager for her mom. Each night, Tonya massaged her mom's feet until she fell asleep. While massaging mom's feet, mom told Tonya about her day and the ongoing fights with Tonya's dad. Tonya constantly reassured her mom that things would ok. "I'm here for you mom. I'm here to do whatever you need to make sure we're ok. Don't worry mom, I'll take care of the house. You just work and pay the bills."

When Tonya becomes an adult, she doesn't understand why she struggles with bouts of anger. She also finds herself pretty annoyed with her mother most of the time. She doesn't take her calls some days because she knows she will want something.

Tonya gets married. When her mother-in-law gets sick and her husband mentions the possibility of he and Tonya taking turns caring for his mom, Tonya loses it and tells her husband that he's being unfair to ask her to take care of his mother. Tonya tells him to either find someone else to take care of his mom or she will move out. Tonya's husband has no idea where this anger and extreme response is coming from. Neither does Tonya.

The "Child Who Became the Parent" syndrome may not sound as bad as "The Trust Buster" or the "I Can Save the World" syndrome. However, like the other two, it can result in unhealthy ways of responding to others and dysfunctional relationships. It becomes a barrier to your loving yourself and living a better life.

Summary:

Although there are many other issues that can affect your self-esteem and relationships, **abandonment (the "Trust Buster"), codependency (the "I Can Save the World" syndrome),** and **parentification (the "Child Becomes the Parent" syndrome)** can have negative effects over the course of a life time without some type of intervention.

Abandonment, codependency, and being parentified affect self-esteem, your sense of value, how you view the world, and how you function in relationships. Their roots can generally be found in one of your earlier relationships (e.g. with a parent/guardian or grandparent) and ultimately continue to infect your relationships. The good news is that when these issues are appropriately addressed, you can have healthy relationships and feel good about yourself.

Self-awareness is one of the keys to understanding why you feel the way you do about yourself and others, why and how you respond to others the way you do, and how you function in relationships (e.g. intimate relationships, with coworkers, family, etc.). Without self-awareness, you may not be clear about your desires, expectations, and the ways in which your experiences have impacted who you are and the decisions you make.

In some cases, it takes others, including trained professionals to help you become more self-aware. As much as you might think you know yourself, if you've had any trauma in your life (e.g., abandonment, rape, molestation, an abusive parent/guardian, major illness, death of a family member or close friend, etc.), it might affect your ability to recognize or identify some of the issues that keep you stuck and unable to love yourself from the inside out. For instance, if you had a parent with an addiction, you might not realize how often you try to rescue others, justify the behavior of others, or the fact that you set really high standards for yourself and others and keep raising the bar each time a standard is met. People close to you might see how dysfunctional your behavior is, but may not tell you unless you ask. In addition, you may not realize the ways in which you keep others from getting close to you or push them away when they start getting close.

What I've described are not healthy behaviors. Whether   it's   abandonment, codependency, parentification, or something else, in order to love yourself from the inside out and have healthy, loving relationships, I believe it is important for you to become aware of the ways in which your past has affected you. After you're aware of the past-present connection, the next step is getting proper support and assistance in addressing any issues. Awareness and support are key to *loving yourself from the inside out* and *becoming a better you.* As you increase your self-awareness, you increase your capacity to open your heart and then you will love yourself and others without fear.

🗝 KEYS FROM THIS CHAPTER

🗝 Your past doesn't have to continue impacting your future

🗝 By addressing issues from your past, you can increase your self-esteem and ability to trust

🗝 Increasing your self-awareness, increases your capacity to love without fear

TIME TO REFLECT

1. Has abandonment, codependency, or parentification been an issue in your life? If yes, which one?

2. Do you find it difficult to trust people or let them get close to you? If yes, what are you afraid of?

3. Under what conditions do you let people get close to you?

4. Do you believe you deserve unconditional love (i.e. love without terms and conditions; without demands and without you having to do something to earn or keep it)?

5. If you really believe you deserve unconditional love, write "I DESERVE UNCONDITIONAL LOVE" below, then say it out loud.

CHAPTER 6

IT'S MUCH GREATER THAN YOU

Love is powerful. When you love yourself, you are powerful. When you love yourself and you are powerful, you will experience life beyond your dreams. (PM Love)

May 20th

Dear Diary,

I can't believe it, but I am seeing a therapist. I thought I'd never go to therapy. I had heard so many negative things about it from family members. I visited 3 different therapists before I found someone I really like and don't mind going to every week. At first when I started going to Dr. Jan, I felt like I was getting worse. She explained that sometimes therapy can be like getting through hard soil. As you start digging below the surface, it can feel a little rough at first, but with a little water and the right tools, it gets easier. Dr. Jan was right and I'm glad I didn't listen to my family.

Over the past few weeks, I've learned a lot about myself and how my past has affected me. I didn't realize how much the divorce of my parents, my mother's health, and my grandfather's addiction had impacted my life. Dr. Jan is helping me learn how to love and take care of myself. I'm learning to be content as a single woman and have started saying "no" to people when they call me to fix their problems. The first time I said no was a little uncomfortable, but now, it feels good!

Dr. Jan has taught me a few anger management techniques. I didn't realize how angry I was.

I've noticed that since I've been dealing with some of my emotional issues, I don't get as many headaches and I'm not as concerned about what other people think about me. This is starting to feel really good.

Dr. Jan asked me what has helped me in the past to get through tough times. I told her I used to pray and go to church. She asked if I thought praying and going back to church might help me on my journey to loving myself and having a better life. I told her I'd think about it and let her know. She gave me an assignment to describe what love is, where it comes from, and what unconditional love means to me. I'd never really given "love" that much thought. This should be interesting.

POINTS TO PONDER

If you've read through each chapter and responded to the questions, you should know some new things about yourself or been reminded of things that you hadn't thought about in a while.

If you completed the exercises at the end of each chapter or at least thought about them, you should know what positive and negative words you use to describe yourself and the ways in which your words/thoughts and the words of others have impacted you. You should also have some understanding of the reasons you have worn a mask and steps you can take so that you feel just as good if not better on the inside than you look when you fix yourself up on the outside.

All of the chapters and questions in this book have been designed to do one thing: help you love yourself without judging yourself so that you can learn to live beyond your dreams.

This journey won't always feel easy or something you want to continue. You may have times when you want to quit. However, becoming more aware of who you are and what influences your thoughts, feelings, and behavior is key to being able to love yourself without a bunch of terms and conditions. When you love yourself unconditionally, you will begin to eliminate toxic people from your life or minimize your interaction with them. You will say "no" a lot more, and you will have more relationships that are healthy and loving.

I've talked a lot about the importance of *loving yourself from the inside out*. In order to do that, you must have an understanding of what love is and what it means to love yourself.

Love is an emotion, a virtue, and action taken to express attachment, commitment or desire. It can be passionate, sensual, unconditional, and so many other things.

Love is considered by some to be the most powerful force in the universe. If you accept this belief, you might also accept that it has a transforming power unlike anything else in the universe. It causes people to act in unexpected ways and experience life through a lens that is clear and focused or cloudy and cracked. Like a mother holding a new born baby or a couple who say they felt love at first sight, love can change your heart and your life.

People have different beliefs about the source of love (e.g. Jesus Christ, God of the universe, Jehovah, Allah, god). I choose to believe that God is love and His love is like nothing and no one in the world. Through His love, I learned that drinking alcohol, smoking cigarettes, getting high, participating in risky sexual activities, and being connected to people who also engaged in risky behaviors was not a life that brought me joy or the fulfillment of things that I hoped to one day achieve. I learned to love myself, get professional help to deal with trauma and other issues from my past, and accepted the support of family, friends, and mentors who could help me along a path to a better life.

As someone who has experienced trauma many times over the course of many years, I understand how hard it is to feel good about yourself. I also understand how the messages from the past and what people say can cause you to have low self esteem, participate in self sabotaging activities, and wear different masks on different days.

I am grateful for God's love and how he did not allow the story of my life to end with my pain. God's love has allowed me to have an amazing journey that overflows with love and so many good things. Love has taught me how to embrace each day with great expectation and a positive attitude. Whenever I start feeling sad or worrying about something or experience other negative emotions, I have learned to pray, read scripture or listen to music to shift me back to a better space. At other times when I begin to slip back into old patterns or start feeling discouraged or stressed, my network of family, friends, and mentors are there to encourage me and remind me of my purpose and God's love. They remind me that I am a loving, caring, gifted woman who is determined to help others who wish to live beyond their dreams. They remind me to be still and listen to God. In that stillness, God reminds me to love from the inside out.

As I have learned to love myself from the inside out, I no longer worry about whether I'm brown enough or if I'm pretty enough. I love myself just the way I am. Now when I put on makeup or fix my hair, I look in the mirror and make sure it's what I want. I no longer compare myself to others or spend time trying to draw attention to myself. I have also learned to laugh at myself, trust myself, and embrace and reveal my authentic self to others. I wish I could tell you I never worry or feel insecure, but that would be a lie. What I can tell you is that on the days I release worry and insecurity, I feel like a bird that was just released from a cage. It's an amazing feeling.

Loving yourself from the inside out requires a certain level of perfection (maturity) and ability to embrace your imperfections (flaws). What does that mean? It means you recognize and accept that because you are human, you will make mistakes. It also means that instead of blaming people or circumstances from your past for your mistakes or challenges, you take responsibility for your life and get help so you can learn what lessons your mistakes may be teaching you.

You should also stop focusing on what you think is wrong. Spend more of your energy acknowledging what is good and learn to recognize when things aren't as bad as they could be. It's like when you have that dreaded hair or blemish under your chin that no one else sees. The blemish could be microscopic, but you notice it and think everyone sees the "big ugly pimple." It's possible that no one notices the pimple until you point it out. The same thing happens when you do or say something that you regret. Let yourself off the hook and try not to beat yourself up. Beating yourself up doesn't make you feel better and it doesn't change what has been done. It only helps you continue feeling bad, guilty, or fearful. It's like you've sentenced yourself to an indefinite emotional punishment. Think about it this way: What if you committed a crime and the prosecuting attorney, judge and jury were the same person? If the prosecutor made up her mind that you were guilty and wanted the jury and judge to agree, you would be found guilty, right? Well that's what emotionally beating yourself up is like. You become the prosecutor, judge and jury. You state the case, provide evidence against yourself, provide testimony after testimony about why you're guilty (in your head of course), give yourself a guilty sentence, and then you serve time (in your head and heart). Love yourself and give yourself a pardon from time to time. Remember, unconditional love forgives and doesn't judge or punish.

Loving yourself from the inside out will take more than you learning to love yourself without conditions, reaching a level of perfection (maturity) and embracing your imperfections (flaws). Just as I have found and maintain a relationship with God, I hope you will discover or embrace a love that is much greater than you. When you embrace love in its fullness, you will see that it is captivating, peaceful, comforting, and can teach you how to love yourself and become your best and highest self. Love will lead you to a life beyond your dreams.

Living beyond your dreams means you achieve things that are far greater and better than you could have expected. It doesn't mean you always get what you want, but you get what you need and what serves you and your purpose. It means you wake up some days and can't believe how different your life is from the way it was in the past. It's not just about having material things (e.g. jewelry, clothing, a house, etc.), it's about feeling like your life is overflowing with great people, amazing opportunities, and the love, peace and joy that your heart has been longing for. This journey is all about love!

🔑 KEYS FROM THIS CHAPTER

- 🔑 Love has a transforming power
- 🔑 Increasing your self-awareness can increase your self-love
- 🔑 Loving yourself requires a level of maturity
- 🔑 Love leads to life beyond your dreams

86 Greater Than You

PART II

CHAPTER 7

EXERCISES FOR A BETTER YOU

What I become will be determined by my thoughts, choices, and actions. How I live each day is up to me. I take full responsibility for my life. I shall live my life with love and joy!
PM Love

PONDER THIS

As you learn to love yourself from the inside out, go easy on yourself. probably won't change overnight. It's possible, but will more than likely take some time.

In this section of the book you will have opportunities to practice taking control of your thoughts and taking steps to identify, visualize, and move forward to the fulfillment of your dreams. The following exercises can help you shift your thinking, affirm what's good about you and your life, and speak positive words for positive results.

Do you really want more out of life? Are you tired of feeling stuck? Do you know that you can do more? Are you willing to do whatever it takes to get more out of life?

If you answered yes to any of the questions and you're very serious, get ready to complete a few practical exercises that can change your life. If you're not serious or if you think you need to go back to previous chapters to review information again, or if you think you might need additional support to address some issues, please know that it's ok. Remember I said that things don't happen overnight? It's true. Just as it took me many years to overcome the pain of my past, I want you to give yourself permission to continue this journey when the time is right. Trust yourself. When you're ready, you'll know.

If you are ready to move forward, get ready to continue on the path to "live beyond your dreams."

Exercises For A Better You!

Questions in previous chapters encouraged you to identify the masks you wear, the positive and negative words you say about yourself and words others spoke to or about you, and how much you are influenced by the words and opinions of others. Some questions were designed to help you examine your thoughts and consider the power of words. Words can be like rain and lightning. They can touch you and dry up without any residual effects. At other times, they hit you, go through you, and can leave long term or permanent damage.

The following exercises are designed to help you increase your self-awareness and affirm some of the things that are good about you and your life. If you're like a lot of people, you spend too much time putting yourself down or magnifying what's not good. It's time for you to shift your mind and focus on what is good, positive, and worthy of being recognized by you and others.

As you complete each exercise, don't be hard on yourself if you find yourself thinking "I don't know the answer to this" or "I'm not there yet." The idea is to take steps that help you work on knowing and loving yourself more than you do now.

If you find yourself stuck and unable to complete the exercises, consider asking others to help you answer some of the questions. After you get answers from others, hold onto them for a day or two. This gives you an opportunity to think about whether their response resonates with you. If it does, go back and complete the exercises in your own words. If their response doesn't resonate, ask someone else who is more likely to be able to share good things they know about you.

> **Note**: Sometimes others see things about you that may be true, but when they tell you, you may not believe that it's true. If you find that different people say some of the same things about you (especially if they know you very well and/or are not likely to be conspiring against you), ask them to elaborate or give you examples to support what they're saying. They may be helping you discover a part of yourself that you weren't aware of.

For each of the following exercises, consider using a journal or notebook to record your responses or type them on your computer.

Exercise #1: Love From The Inside Out

Directions: Fill in each of the blanks:

1. Of all of my features, I love my
   _____ the most.

2. I also like my _____.

3. I accept that I am unique (different).
   One thing I'm really good at is
   _____.

4. I enjoy doing the following:
   _____
   _____

5. I have done some good things. One
   that I'm proud of is when I
   _____
   _____

6. When I look at myself in the mirror, I
   see someone who is beautiful and

   _____.

7. Although some things have happened
   in my past, I look forward to a future
   that is full of/or to have more of:

   _____

   _____.

Exercise #2: Truth or Perception

Directions: Write a story about your life. Start from when you were a child or when you were a teenager or talk about your life now. After you complete the story, go back and underline what is true and put a circle or box around what is your opinion, perception, or someone else's opinion or belief.

This exercise will help you begin to look at how much of what you say, think, and feel is based in truth and how much is based in perception, fear, and things that you either make up or buy into as being true when it is not. Look at the sample story below and then write your own story.

Sample story for Exercise #2

I was born on a Sunday morning to a mother who didn't want me. I was the youngest of 7. They said my mother didn't want me because she couldn't afford to feed one more child. So she gave me to a family who only wanted me for the money they got from the state. I hated growing up with my adopted parents. They didn't know how to deal with me. After graduating high school, I got my own place and have been on my own ever since. My parents didn't even care enough for me to give me a housewarming or buy furniture for my place. They probably used money they could have spent on me for a vacation or something else for themselves. I haven't had a stable relationship and keep meeting men who try to take advantage of me. I also don't have a lot of close friends and I definitely don't get close to female because they are caddy and you can't be trusted.

Sample story – Checking truth vs. perception. This version of the story has been completed to show you what to do:

Underline=truth statement   Circle or box around the word(s)=my perception or opinion

I was <u>born on a Sunday</u> morning to a mother who didn't want me. I was <u>the youngest of 7</u>. They said my mother didn't want me because she couldn't afford to feed one more child. So she gave me to a family who only wanted me for the money they got from the state. <u>I hated growing up</u> with my adopted parents. They didn't know how to deal with me. After graduating high school, <u>I got my own place and have been on my own ever since</u>. My parents didn't even care enough for me to give me a housewarming or buy furniture for my place. They probably used money they could have spent on me for a vacation or something else for themselves. I haven't had a stable relationship and keep meeting men who try to take advantage of me. I also don't have a lot of close friends and I definitely don't get close to female because they are caddy and you can't be trusted.

(Can you tell what else in the sample is true vs. a perception or opinion?) If you haven't done so already, write your own story and then go back and underline what is true and circle or put a box around your perception or opinion.

Exercise #3: Encouraging Myself

Directions: Write a letter to yourself to encourage yourself. When you finish writing the letter, put it in an envelope and write your mailing address on it. Also put a return address on the envelope. Seal the envelope, put a stamp on it, and give it to someone who you trust. Ask the person to mail it to you at some time in the future. The idea is for it to arrive in your mail when you least expect it.

Frequently when people complete this exercise, they say they receive the letter on a day when they needed to be encouraged or at a time when it confirms what they're trying to do.

Remember, this is your letter to yourself. Say things that are positive and encouraging. Say things that may not be true at the moment, but that you hope to see in the future. You can make it as long as you'd like. It's your letter. Also feel free to draw pictures on the letter or to write it using crayons. If you prefer to type it, that's fine. Do whatever you think will bring a smile to your face when you receive the letter in the mail, open the envelope and read a letter you wrote that is full of encouraging words.

Here's a sample letter that a young woman wrote who had been abandoned by her dad and struggled to have healthy relationships:

Sample for Exercise #3: "Encouraging Myself"

July 2, 2011

Dear Renee:

When you looked in the mirror today, I know you saw that beautiful smile that lights up your face. I hope you also saw someone whose life overflows with love and joy. You have so many people in your life who love you unconditionally. Isn't it wonderful that you can trust them and feel safe and secure in their presence? You are so fortunate to have close friends who don't stab you in the back and who look out for you.

You are an encouragement to others and you cook better than anyone I know. Your food is so delicious. You are talented and gifted. When you dance, you do it so gracefully. It's like you and the song become one. You're such a giving person, but you also know how to take care of yourself. I love that about you. You know how to say no without making excuses, but you also do things that make people feel special. You have a high self-esteem and you allow yourself to trust and be vulnerable in relationships.

I want you to know how much I love and how proud of you I am for all of the things you've overcome and how you've turned the onions in your life into French onion soup. You are unstoppable. Like an eagle, you continue to soar and will no doubt, soar higher and higher. I love you, girl.

Love and hugs,

Me☺

Exercise #4: I Love Me Exercise

Directions: Read the following message three or more times in a row. Read it every day until you believe every word. Encourage others to read it also

Are you ready? It's time you believe the following:

I entered the world at the right time. I had the parents/caretakers I was supposed to have and was born exactly where and how I was supposed to be born. My life was no accident.

In spite of all I've gone through, I'm still alive. That's because there is a purpose for my life. No one can do what I was born to do exactly like me. That's why I am a designer's original.

I love me just the way I am. Although I'm not perfect (without flaws), I am perfect (mature). I love me and know that it's ok when I make

mistakes. I learn from my mistakes and they help me do better the next time. I love that I am not a quitter. I hang in there when things get tough because I know that tough times are temporary. I love that I don't compare myself to others or think that I'm better than others. I am who I am and will not be influenced by the opinions of others. I know that what I think of myself is more important than what others think of me.

I love my life. I trust myself and therefore have allowed people to be close to me that love and respect me. They celebrate me instead of tolerating me. They are people who have similar values. They love themselves too.

Today I embrace who I am, who I was created to be, and what I am here to give to the world. I am full of love, overflowing with joy, and filling up on the good that is in my life and that will be coming.

I love me. Because of my unconditional love for myself, I show up in the world without masks or fear. I don't seek attention or do things that are self-sabotaging or damaging to other people or my relationships. I am an expression of love. As I give to others, I continue to receive in abundance. I achieve beyond my wildest dreams.

I love me and there's nothing anyone can do about it!

Exercise #5: Achieving Beyond My Dreams (Writing Your Goal Statement)

Living a life that overflows with love starts with your thoughts. Your thoughts affect your emotions. Your emotions affect your decisions. Your decisions affect your actions.

As you embrace who you are, love yourself unconditionally, become more self-aware, and release negative emotions, you will be more confident and able to do things you may not have been able to do in the past. You will position yourself to achieve beyond your wildest dreams.

To help you on this journey, below is an exercise you can use when you're ready to take a step to achieve one or more of your goals.

Take a second and think about some things you want to do. For instance, you might want to return to school to get a degree. What about the dream you recently shared with a friend to open a home for women who are released from prison? What about your goal of traveling to Paris or the Bahamas or take a cruise? What about writing a book or taking cake decorating classes? Learning Spanish? Going to Africa? Starting your own business?

Write down everything that comes to mind. For this exercise, pick one of your dreams/desires/goals. Stop for a second. Are you thinking that what you've written down is too big? You don't have the resources for it? It's something you'll never do? If so, shut those thoughts down immediately. Replace them with positive thoughts. Speak to your mind and tell it that if this is something you really want to do, no matter how big or small the goal is, you can achieve it. When you believe it, at some point you will be able to visualize it as if it has already happened. Try that for a second. Close your eyes and imagine yourself just completing your goal. What does that feel like? It might feel a little scary, but it should make you smile or feel good. When you're able to visualize your goal/dream being fulfilled, your mind will subconsciously start moving you in that direction. Before you know it, you will be saying "I've achieved my goal." It's a great feeling to accomplish something you've been thinking about or have told others you want to accomplish. It's an even better feeling when it turns out better than you ever imagined!

To help you on your journey of having a life that overflows with love – one in which you have joy, love yourself unconditionally, and are achieving your goals, I have created the following exercise. If you read the message in

Exercise #4 over and over along with the goal statement that you will create, your life will never be the same. Why? Because not only will you feel like you have a full tank of love, you will begin to achieve beyond your dreams like so many people are doing right now. You will no longer wish you could have a different life, it will happen.

Directions: On a sheet of paper or on your computer, complete the following (If you'd like or if it's easier, skip to the next few pages for a sample goal statement that has been completed for you) :

By _____(fill in the month, day & year), I will _____(fill in something you've been wanting to do).

Here are reasons why I haven't done this already: _____(These are the real or made up excuses you've told yourself). Fill in every obstacle, emotion, or reason you believe you haven't done what you wanted to do. It could be money, a person, fear, you didn't know how to do it, you didn't think you had time, or other reasons).

I will not allow the reasons I listed above to stop me from achieving my goals anymore. I will reach out to _____(identify at least 2-3 people who can support you in reaching your goal(s). These should be people you believe can help you and will hold you accountable. They can help you identify the steps necessary to achieve your goal and help you develop an action plan. They should also be people who will encourage you and who have accomplished what you'd like to accomplish or something similar.

Don't worry about whether or not the 2-3 people will support you in this process. This is where you must learn to trust that the right people will help you in the right time if you really want the help and really want to achieve your goal. Don't get anxious or give in to your fear. Trust that whoever comes to mind when you think about people who will support you are the right people or they can direct you to the right people.

I trust that the two or three people I've identified will either provide support, encouragement, and/or guidance in the process of fill in your goal OR they will direct me to the resources to help me fill in your goal.

When I _____ (fill in your goal), I will _____(list how you will feel, what you will do to celebrate, who you will tell, etc.).

If I have any days when I doubt that I will achieve my goal, I will: 1. _____ (list someone you can call, an affirmation, scripture, or message you can read or a song you can listen to that will give you the motivation you need. You can list several things you will do. Different things might work during different times).

I commit to this goal, am excited about achieving this goal, and look forward to celebrating the achievement of this goal.

<u>Sign your name this letter.</u>   <u>Put the date you wrote</u>

On the next few pages is an example of what your document might look like. It is only an example and doesn't haven't to be done in exactly the same way. Your document should reflect you 100%.

Sample Goal Statement:

By <u>December 31, 2012,</u> I will <u>complete the</u> <u>book that I started in 2011 and have been</u> <u>wanting to complete</u>.

The reasons I haven't <u>completed my book</u> include: 1. <u>I wasn't sure what to put in each</u> <u>chapter; 2. I started working a part-time job and</u> <u>never seemed to have time; 3. I don't feel like</u> <u>I'm a good writer; 4. My friend told me that</u> <u>nobody would be interested in reading the book</u> <u>that I said I wanted to write.</u>

I will not allow the reasons I listed above to stop me from achieving my goals anymore. I will reach out to <u>Jennifer, Dr. Robinson, and</u> <u>Cynthia</u>. I trust that one or all three of them will either provide support, encouragement, and/or guidance in the process of <u>completing my book</u> OR one or all three of them will direct me to the resources that helps me <u>complete my book</u>.

When I complete my book, I will be so proud of myself. I will celebrate by going out to dinner with family/friends; I will let others know what I have accomplished and what it took to finish my book.

If I have any days when I doubt that I will achieve my goal, I will: 1. Call someone who will encourage me; 2. Read an affirmation; 3. Keep reminding myself that I have everything I need to achieve my goal.

I commit to this goal, am excited about achieving this goal, and look forward to celebrating the achievement of this goal.

Jessica R. Friend   July 3, 2012

You can use the above exercise for as many goals as you'd like to achieve.

After you write your goal statement, take a sheet of paper and type or write the following in really big letters:

"I ACHIEVED MY GOAL"

Follow the instructions in Exercise 6.

Exercise #6: "I Achieved My Goal"

Take a picture of yourself smiling as if you just won the lottery and holding the piece of paper with "I ACHIEVED MY GOAL" on it. You can also find a picture that represents your goal (e.g. a house; a car; a book, going back to school, etc.) or a combination of things you want to achieve and put the pictures onto a sheet of paper or poster board. Be sure to put the picture of you smiling next to it.

What I just described can be the beginning of a vision board. If you're interested in learning more about vision boards, search for information and resources on the internet. Creating a vision board is a powerful activity for visualizing what you intend to have or accomplish. It can trick the mind into believing the goal is already achieved and cause you to take steps that lead to completion of what's on the board.

CHAPTER 8

TIME FOR NEW BEGINNINGS

The clock is ticking. That's a good sign you see. That means I still have some time to become a better me. My dreams have been patiently waiting. I'm so glad they're still alive. I believe they will come to fruition now that I have the vision, determination and drive.

---PM Love

PONDER THIS

By now you should have discovered some things about yourself, what you need to do to become a better you, and live beyond your dreams.

Here's the bottom line: How you live your life is up to you. You can continue to wear a mask and struggle with issues from your past or you can learn to love yourself from the inside out and live beyond your dreams. You can stay where you are and complain or like an eagle, flap your wings and take flight.

I know it's not as easy as I make it sound, but it is possible. It's possible if you decide to learn the lessons from your past, become more self-aware and responsible for your decisions and actions, and if you believe and take steps described in this book to become a better you. With the right support and a determination that is unyielding, you will achieve your dreams and live a more joyful life.

As you prepare to experience new beginnings, there is one final thing to consider. That is whether or not there are people you need to forgive. Are there people who hurt you, abused you, or did something that resulted in your experiencing bouts of anger, feelings of resentment, or depression? It's normal to have negative feelings and emotions when something bad happens to you. However, holding on to those negative feelings is unhealthy and can cause emotional and physical health problems that can be costly for you and people around you.

If you answered yes, you may be wondering what you need to do next. The answer is simple: forgive. Am I serious? Yes. Forgiving someone who did something bad to you is liberating and helps you move forward without frequent glances in the rear view mirror of life. Forgiveness is really about releasing the negative emotions you experience when you think about the person or situation that resulted in you feeling hurt or angry. To release those emotions, keep reminding yourself that although what happened in the past may have been mean, sick, painful, unnecessary, or ruthless, you will no longer allow it to control your life. Decide that you will no longer let your thoughts and emotions be consumed by the past. Refuse to give the keys to your future to a situation or person from your past that you are emotionally connected to.

It's easy to get stuck, keep thinking about your past, and continue blaming others for why you're where you are. That may be ok for a while. However, as you mature, you learn to stop making excuses, let go of the past, and make the most of today. I'm not saying that you will or should forget what happened in your past. It is part of what has influenced who and what you have become. I'm suggesting that you release any negativity, accept that there's nothing you can do to change the past, and decide that you will make the most of today. You might not ever forget your past. It is part of your life and your story. Let it push you forward. Allow it to teach you lessons that you can use to help someone else. Instead of letting it cripple you, cause shame, guilt, and drive you to self-sabotaging behaviors (e.g. overeating, cutting, risky sexual activities, excessive alcohol and drug use, etc.), let your past be like a wind that lifts you up and helps you soar with excitement and expectation of great things to come.

I want you to soar like an eagle and believe you are a gift to someone. I want you to fix yourself up on the outside, but do it because you feel like it not because you need to so you can feel better or you think it's the only way to attract someone's attention. I want you to have relationships that allow you to open your arms instead of folding them and pushing people away. I want you to accept that if you were abandoned or became codependent or parentified, it wasn't your fault. I want you to believe that everyone won't hurt you or need you to take care of them in unhealthy ways. I want you to eat for health and not to comfort yourself. I really want the best for you.

If you want to become a better you and live beyond your dreams, believe that you can, embrace the support to help you get there, and go do it!

Remember that this book was not designed to provide all of the answers you need. It was designed to help you become more aware of some things that may be holding you back and to give you practical steps you can take to discover some things about yourself in order to have a better life.

Don't forget to contact the people you identified in Exercise #5 and ask for their support. These individuals can hold you accountable, help you when you aren't sure what to do, and may be able to identify resources you need to achieve your goal(s). You should also consult a trained professional for guidance and support if you feel you want to talk privately with someone who can be objective and help you explore some issues further.

I hope this is a season of new beginnings for you. Don't forget to go back and read exercise #4 over and over until you believe it. You can also create your own affirmation or use one that you found in another book. Whatever you use, be sure to post it where you will see it and read it daily. Also remember to post the picture of you with your goal statement. If you did not complete exercise #6, go back and complete it.

Life is a journey full of some things you can control and some things you have no control over. There will always be highs and lows, sunshine and rain. The highs give you hope. The lows can reveal areas where you need to mature or how much you've grown. Lows also help you appreciate the highs in life. The sun will burn some things out of your life that aren't good; the rain will cause some things to grow and can cleanse your life and thoughts. You see, it's all about perspective. That's what **learning to love yourself from the inside** out is all about.

Dr. Pam Love

CONTACTING DR. PAM LOVE

Dr. Pam Love welcomes your feedback regarding how this book impacted your life. To share a testimonial about this book or to invite Dr. Love to speak at one of your events:

Email: drpamlove@gmail.com

Mail: PM Love Enterprises
            PO Box 47133
            Baltimore, MD 21244
Phone: 240 242-9555

Other books by Dr. Pam Love:

It's All About Love: Living Your Purpose In Spite of Your Past

I Want My Vagina Back (book and journal. The book is also available on audio and e-readers)

To find out how you can order additional products and services and to see what else Dr. Love is doing, visit www.drpamlove.com.

Made in the USA
Charleston, SC
28 October 2012